Behavior Principles

Core Classroom Management Knowledge for Educators

3rd Edition

Yadira Flores, Ph.D.
Daniel Gulchak, Ph.D.
Angel Jannasch-Pennell, Ph.D.
Birgit Lurie, BCBA

www.KOI-Education.com

KOI Education Behavior Principles, 3rd Edition

ISBN-13: 978-0-9883118-6-2 (eBook)
ISBN-13: 978-0-9883118-7-9 (Paperback)

eBook available for purchase online.

© 2012–2019 KOI Education

All rights reserved. No part of this book may be reproduced or utilized in any form or by any means, electronic or mechanical, including photocopying, recording, or by an information storage and retrieval system without the permission in writing from the authors.

Purchasers of this book are granted permission for educational purpose to photocopy and use blank forms, checklist, and action planning documents in the book. Materials are not authorized to be used by other commercial entities or for commercial purposes.

All documents available from KOI-Education.com website are licensed under a Creative Commons Attribution-NonCommercial-ShareAlike 3.0 Unported License.

TABLE OF CONTENTS

Learning Objectives: 5

Defining Behavior Principles 5

Identify Form and Function of Behavior 6

    The Form of Behavior 6

    The Function of Behavior 7

    Define The Form of Behavior with Precision 9

Setting Expectations 10

Providing Reinforcement 11

    Reinforcement Myths: 13

    Shaping a New Behavior 15

    Reinforcing Behavior Effectively 17

Consistent Accountability 17

Conclusion 20

Review 21

Acknowledgments 22

Our Organization 23

Notes 26

"If there is anything we wish to change in the child, we should first examine it and see whether it is not something that could better be changed in ourselves."

—Carl Jung

Learning Objectives:

1. Defining Behavior Principles
2. Identify Form and Function of Behavior
3. Setting Expectations
4. Providing Reinforcement
5. Consistent Accountability

DEFINING BEHAVIOR PRINCIPLES

When we understand Behavior Principles, we can modify behaviors we seek to change. Knowing Behavior Principles is a prerequisite for choosing effective interventions. Let's start by talking about Behavior. Behavior is the activity of all living organisms. It encompasses what we do, what we say, what we feel and what we think. Behavior is not static but can be described using a verb. Behavior does not describe a state of mind such as being happy, angry, bored or excited, but rather what we do when we are in that particular state of mind. *"She jumped up and down and clapped her hands when she saw her team score a goal"*. This is a description of the behavior (*clapped and jumped*) indicating that she is excited (*state of mind*).

Principles of Behavior are the science of human behavior. These behavior principles have four components:

1. Behavior is a product of its immediate environment:
   a. A teacher compliments a student's performance and the student smiles. The smile occurs as a response to the immediate environment—the teacher's compliment.
   b. It starts to rain, and you open an umbrella. Opening an umbrella is the behavioral response to the immediate environment—the rain.
2. Behavior is strengthened or weakened by its consequences:
   a. A student raises his hand and the teacher compliments the student for remembering to raise his hand. In the future the student is more likely to continue raising his hand because the teacher complimented him. The compliment caused the behavior to increase.

b. A toddler touches a hot oven door and cries because it hurts. In the future the toddler is likely to avoid the oven door. The pain caused the behavior of touching the door to decrease.
c. Student A starts teasing Student B about what she is wearing. Student B ignores Student A's comments. Student B's lack of response and ignoring the teasing behavior causes the teasing behavior to stop.
3. Behavior can be observed and measured in terms of frequency, duration and intensity:
   a. Sarah completed 15 jumping jacks. (Frequency)
   b. Joe ran for 15 minutes. (Duration)
   c. Carol pinched Ben on the arm so forcefully that a red mark could be seen two hours later. (Intensity).
4. Behavior has a Form and a Function:
   a. All behavior has a Form (What the behavior looks like)
   b. All behavior has a Function (The Purpose of the Behavior)

....

IDENTIFY FORM AND FUNCTION OF BEHAVIOR

The Form of Behavior

Consider a Middle School Girl Screaming.

What should you do?

Most teachers would answer, "It depends". And that is absolutely correct. Clearly, we can't answer this question yet because there are too many unknowns. All we know is what we can see: The physical FORM of the behavior, what the behavior looks like. In this case, the form of the behavior is screaming. We can describe the screaming, we can state how loud and how long the screaming is. But we need to understand 'why' the behavior is occurring in order to be able to change the behavior. To solve behavior problems, we must act on the FUNCTION of the behavior which is 'behavioral speak' for the why of the behavior. The function of behavior can also be thought of as the reason or purpose for the behavior. Interventions are based on function not form.

The Function of Behavior

Most school behavior has one of two functions:

1. **Get Something:** Task/Activity/Object, Attention (adult/peers), Sensory/Stimulation
2. **Avoid Something:** Task/Activity/Object, Attention(adult/peers), Sensory/Stimulation

The flowchart shows how we look at a behavior and then decide, based on observation and input from people who know the student, whether the behavior in question occurs because the student wants something or is avoiding something. We then determine what it is they want to get or avoid.

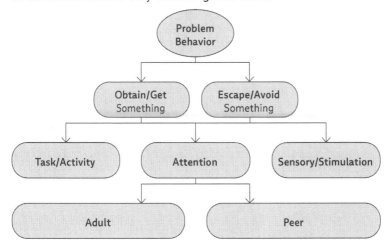

Once we determine the function or the why of the behavior, we can then develop an effective intervention plan to teach the student how to get or avoid something, using more appropriate behaviors.

Let's take a look at three possible functions for the middle school girl who is screaming:

- "Gimmie, I want that book now" (get something)
- "Go away, I don't want to write an essay" (avoid something)
- "Ouch, a wasp just stung me." (sensory)

Our intervention will be different for each scenario above because the Function is different. Let's take a look:

- Let's say the student screams to get the book for her project, the function of screaming is to get something they want or need, but the behavior is inappropriate. So what should we do? In order for the intervention to be effective we must address the function. An effective intervention for this example would be to teach her appropriate ways to get the book, such as teaching her how to ask for the book, " Can I have the book please?". This would meet her behavioral need for getting something, but in an acceptable manner.

- What if the student screams when presented with a writing assignment to avoid the task. What should we do? We could find out why she is avoiding writing assignments. She may have difficulty spelling, she may only be able to write one paragraph, writing may be strenuous for her or she may not like to write. Once we can find out why the student has a need to avoid the task, we then can identify some skills to teach to help address her difficulty with writing, such as asking for a break, we can identify some reinforcers, or modify the activity by allowing her to use a computer and make the activity more pleasant. But before we decide what to do, we first need to understand the function of the behavior, the why?

- What if the student screams because she got stung by a wasp and it hurts. This is a sensory issue and an expected response. We can help the student by sending her to the nurse and we do not need to change the behavior.

Although in the scenarios above, the form of the behavior is the same, screaming, the intervention you choose will be different for each scenario based on the why or function of the behavior. Remember, the intervention must serve the same purpose: getting something, avoiding something, or meeting a sensory need. If the function of the behavior is to get something, then the replacement behavior must also be designed to get something. If the behavior is to avoid something, then the intervention must teach the student how to appropriately avoid something. The same applies to a sensory need.

 All behavior has a form and a function. Take a look at the Tantrum Video at: youtu.be/Gk-OfmmRaqs

The video shows a toddler rolling on the floor and screaming. However, whenever the parents move from the toddler's sight, he stops screaming, walks over to where the parents can see him, and then resumes his tantrum. This makes it easy to identify that the Form of the behavior (what we see) is screaming, while the Function of the behavior (the purpose, the reason, the why), seems to be to get the attention of a parent. If we want to change a behavior we need to figure out why it occurs in the first place (Function). But just as important as identifying the function of behavior, we must also be able to define the behavior with precision (Form) so we can measure it and monitor change over time.

Define The Form of Behavior with Precision

Behaviors are often described in very general terms. Here are some examples:
- "He is so nice and considerate"
- "She drives me crazy every day"
- "They never do their homework"
- "Given her poor attention, no wonder she always fails test"
- "He is a reliable and diligent student"
- "He tantrums every day"

Statements like "He is so nice and considerate" and "She drives me crazy every day" describe a person, not a behavior. This is OK in conversation, but not productive if we want to change a behavior.

The statements, "They never do their homework" and "He tantrums every day" are indeed descriptions of actual behavior, but the statements are vague and imprecise. If we use vague and imprecise behavioral descriptors, we will experience difficulty getting precise data on how often the behavior occurs, for how long the behavior occurs and how intense the behavior is. For more information on collecting behavioral data and data tracking tools, please refer to the KOI PBIS Tier 3 manual. If the form of the behavior is not defined with precision, it is difficult to identify the correct function or reason why the behavior is occurring. Without an accurate form and function we will not be able to effectively change the behavior. Behavior needs to be defined in specific, objective and descriptive terms. For example:

- When Bob throws objects, screams in a loud voice, kicks objects it is defined as tantrum behavior.

Reflection: Take a moment to reflect on Form and Function of behavior.

- Think of an example of a common disruptive school behavior you have seen and define the form with precision and identify the function of that behavior.
- Think of a replacement behavior that would serve the same function.

SETTING EXPECTATIONS

To be effective in increasing, decreasing or changing behavior we must describe a behavior with precision stated in specific, objective and descriptive terms.

Let's look at an example of a vague behavioral descriptor changed to a precise behavioral statement:

- Sarah is safe—Sarah is safe when she keeps her hands, feet and objects to self.

When we use precise behavioral statements all school staff can answer yes or no when asked whether Sarah is safe. This is extremely important because it is the foundation for a consistent and agreed upon response to a behavior. When all staff respond consistently when Sara is unsafe, the behavior will change more quickly.

We can use this behavior principle to increase positive behaviors school-wide by creating precise agreed upon behavioral expectations. Below is an example of precisely defined school behaviors from a school that implements positive behavior intervention and supports (PBIS). PBIS is a framework that guides selection, organization and implementation of evidence-based practices based on behavior principles. A similar expectations matrix could easily be developed for home or any residential setting. By creating and defining behavioral expectations schools can then provide direct teaching of those behaviors, reinforce those behaviors and correct the inappropriate behavior. For more information about creating and defining school-wide behavioral expectations please refer to the KOI PBIS Tier 1 Manual.

See a good example of an Expectation Matrix on the next page.

....

PROVIDING REINFORCEMENT

Reinforcement is anything added immediately after a behavior that causes the behavior to be maintained or increased. Behavior theory postulates that if a person's behavior is not maintained or increased, then whatever was added is not a reinforcement or a reinforcer. This theory has been scientifically proven in thousands of experimental studies in all types of educational settings across the globe.

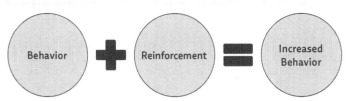

Sacaton Elementary School
Expectation Matrix - 3 Be's

	Be Respectful	Be Responsible	Be Safe
Classrooms	· Be polite and courteous · Use inside voices	· Be on time · Be prepared · Be on task · Use and care for equipment/ materials	· Sit correctly · Always walk · Keep hands, feet and objects to yourself
Playground	· Be polite and courteous · Include and allow everyone to play	· Use and care for equipment/ materials · Line up when whistle blows	· Ask permission to leave the playground · Use playground safely · Keep hands, feet and objects to yourself · Leave rocks/sand on the ground
Cafeteria	· Stand in line and wait your turn · Be polite and courteous · Use inside voices	· Keep your area clean · Raise hand to leave table	· Sit facing your table · Always walk · Keep hands, feet and objects to yourself
Walkways	· Be polite and courteous · Use inside voice	· Go straight to your new location · Have a hall pass	· Always walk · Keep hands, feet and objects to yourself
Bathroom	· Be polite and courteous · Use inside voices	· Flush, wash, dry, goodbye · Report any issues	· Always walk · Keep hands, feet and objects to yourself
Bus	· Listen and follow adult directions · Use courteous and appropriate language · Use inside voices	· Enjoy your food and drinks before you board the bus · Be on time for bus pick up · Keep surfaces graffiti-free	· Keep hands, feet and objects to self and inside the bus · Always remain seated · Enter/exit in orderly fashion · Enjoy electronic devices off the bus

The most important behavioral concept to understand about reinforcement is that reinforcement can be used to maintain or increase any behavior. For example:
- Raising a hand to ask a question is reinforced by the teacher answering the question
- Getting all trigonometry questions correct on a final exam is reinforced with an A+ or a 4.0 GPA
- Showing up at work every day is reinforced with a paycheck

 The first part of this video illustrates reinforcement in action: youtu.be/JA96Fba-WHks

Some educators may not be aware that they are already using reinforcement in the form of giving stickers, check marks, positive feedback and grades to increase academic skills and that they can also use these same reinforcement principles to increase behavior skills. Let's explore some persistent myths about reinforcement that may cause educators to be reluctant to use these principles in school.

Reinforcement Myths:

- Reinforcement and reward are the same
- Reinforcing students spoil them
- Reinforcing students is bribery
- Reinforcing students reduces intrinsic motivation
- Reinforcement costs too much time and money

There is no evidence in scientific literature that supports these myths.

- Reinforcement and rewards are not the same. Rewards are not earned—people often get rewarded whether they earned it or not. Consider the bank executive who gets a bonus even during an economic recession. Reinforcement is earned—like grades, a paycheck or a compliment. Rewards are given to people, reinforcement is given to behaviors.

- Reinforcement does not spoil students. Reinforcement is an acknowledgment of what a student is doing right, so the behavior is repeated in the future. In schools, students are given a number of reinforcers such as earning a letter grade of "A", check mark, star, sticker, happy face, or 100% in response to a correct answer on an assignment, test or quiz. Providing students with acknowledgment/reinforcement for appropriate academic behavior (providing correct answer) does not spoil students, it lets them know they gave the correct answer so they are more likely to repeat that same correct response in the future. There is no difference between reinforcing academic behavior (correct answer) and reinforcing social behavior (following directions, being on task.)

- Reinforcement is not bribery when used correctly. Bribery is used to coerce students. Telling students they can receive 5 tickets for picking up trash is coercion and bribery—this is not reinforcement. Coercion, like punishment, is not effective in the long run. A reinforcement system is not coercion because it's a planned acknowledgment of specific desired behaviors.

- The most concerning myth about reinforcement is that it will reduce student's intrinsic motivation. According to research, the opposite appears to be true. Research findings suggest that reinforcement maintains intrinsic motivation for students who are already intrinsically motivated and increases intrinsic motivation for those students who lack it (Perez, H.,1998, Cameron, Banko and Pierce, 2001).

- Reinforcement does not cost too much time and money. Time can be wasted giving attention to inappropriate behaviors which will reinforce those behaviors or we can spend the time to reinforce the desired behavior which will increase the frequency of those behaviors. We choose how to spend the time. In regards to cost, reinforcement does not have to be expensive. There are hundreds of free and inexpensive ways to acknowledge and reinforcement students for appropriate behaviors. Here are some examples:
    » Consumables (food, sticker, pencil, ticket or a drawing)
    » Activities (recess, board game, computer time)
    » Social Interaction ("good job", thumbs up, line leader)
    » Manipulative's (stress ball, elastic, play clay)
    » Possessions (stuffed animal, teacher's pointer, class ball)
    » Academic Tasks (activity stations, reading in rocking chair, chess, math game, extra time to research on computer)

We recommend the ebook *Having Fun with PBIS: Free or No-cost Reinforcers for Appropriate Behavior* by Dr. Laura Riffel BehaviorDoctorPublications.com filled with over 76 pages of ideas and examples from schools.

Shaping a New Behavior

 We can shape new behaviors by using the same principles for increasing a behavior, take a look at this video: youtu.be/c_0bhT98g9Y

Shaping is a process of reinforcing behaviors the child can do, and then progressively changing the behavior that is reinforced using small steps until a new behavior is achieved. Let's see how the behavior in the video example was unintentionally shaped using reinforcement.

1. The first time the child went to the market with Dad and requested candy, Dad said "No", so the Child started begging and pouting then Dad gave him the candy.
2. Next time they went to the market, the child asked for candy but Dad said "No", he begged and pouted but Dad continue to say "No, not this time". The Child screamed and refused to put the candy back, so Dad went ahead and gave him the candy to make him stop.
3. Again when the Child and Dad went to the Market, the child asked for candy, Dad thought this time I will not give in, so when the Child asked for candy he refused, Child screamed and refused to put the candy back and Dad continued to say "No", so Child started shaking the shopping cart while screaming, Dad then said "Okay stop, you can have the candy".

As you can see with this example, giving the candy was reinforcing the behavior and a new behavior was shaped. Many times we unintentionally shape inappropriate or undesired behaviors by being unaware that we are reinforcing the behavior. Shaping is a process of reinforcing successive approximations to develop a new behavior. We can use reinforcement to Shape a desired new behavior. Take a look at the examples below:

- A young child learning to talk is a good example of shaping. Learning to say the name "Andrew" is difficult for a little one. The first attempt may be just "Ah". The child is reinforced then the correct pronunciation is modeled. After a while the little one says "Andu" and then only that pronunciation is reinforced while "Ah" is ignored. Again, after some modeling the little one finally says "Andrew" and now only the correct pronunciation is reinforced while "Andu" is ignored.

- Consider a scenario where we want a student to be responsible and come to class when the bell rings. If the student has never demonstrated this independently, we might follow these steps to Shape the new behavior of coming inside when the bell rings.
    a. Reinforce the student for coming inside with the teacher when the teacher goes to the playground and reminds him that recess is over and it is time to come in.
    b. Reinforce the student for coming inside when the teacher calls his name from the doorway at the end of recess to remind him that recess is over and it is time to come in.
    c. Reinforce the student when the bell rings and he comes inside with all the other students.

Shaping is an appropriate teaching technique when we want to teach a new behavior. Here are some tips:

- Begin with the end in mind, identify the final desired behavior.
- Start with a behavior that the child can do.
- Take small steps—if the child stops responding, assess whether the reinforcement is reinforcing for the child or go back a step and take it a little slower.
- Be careful, children can shape our behavior too.

The image below is a graphic representation of this principle.

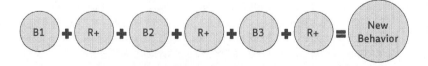

Reinforcing Behavior Effectively

Reinforcement is most effective when it immediately follows the behavior we wish to increase. It's important to be specific and state the actual behavior when reinforcing. For example:

- Thank you for being respectful, I like the way you are following my directions.
- I like the way you are being safe by keeping your hand, and feet to yourself.
- I appreciate you arriving to class on time, thank you for being responsible.

Research has shown that teachers who use reinforcement more often than correction, are more likely to see a decrease in problem behaviors. The optimum reinforcement ratio is 5:1, meaning five positive comments for every one correction. For more information about reinforcement and how to create a school-wide reinforcement system please refer to the KOI PBIS Tier 1 Manual.

Remember:

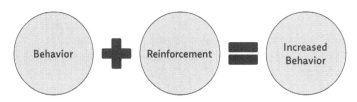

CONSISTENT ACCOUNTABILITY

Some might say that without punishment there is no consequence. Indeed, there should be accountability and consequences when students at school or children at home do not follow agreed upon expectations, but that does not necessarily equate to punishment. It is faulty to equate punishment with consequences. Consequence is just what happens after a behavior occurs. Reinforcement and re-teaching is a consequence.

If an adult in the cafeteria sees a student staying in his or her seat, the adult can say, "Thank you for being safe by staying in your seat". This specific praise is a consequence for following cafeteria behavior expectations. Because the consequence is reinforcement, it is likely that the student will continue to exhibit safe behavior. Remember, reinforcement maintains or increase behavior.

If a student does not exhibit the agreed upon behavioral expectations, we need to provide agreed upon consequences that the student knows and is familiar with. The behavioral flowchart on the following page illustrates how it is possible to address behavioral infractions in an instructional manner with the goal being to prevent the behavior from occurring in the future.

The behavioral flowchart clearly outlines consequences for not following school expectations, but the consequence is focused on changing the behavior by reminding the student what the expectations are, by reteaching the expected behavior and by having the student reflect on their behavior before a staff managed behavior turns into an office discipline referral (ODR). For more serious infractions which are managed by the administrator of the school, the policy of the district is followed.

Behavioral flowcharts like this one can be adapted to the home setting, residential setting and other settings outside the school environment. To learn more about creating a behavior flowchart please refer to the KOI PBIS Tier 1 Manual.

Consequence for not following expectations should be consistent and focus on behavior change through teaching and reinforcement of the desired behavior. This leads to a positive environment where students feel safe and supported. Research consistently shows that this approach leads to positive behavior change. Punishment in the form of seclusion and suspension rarely leads to long term behavior change.

....

MOHAVE BEHAVIOR DISCIPLINE CHART

Problem behavior is observed

Is the behavior office managed? (see chart below) — **No** → Use Minor Behavior/Intervention Tracking Sheet - One sheet per behavior

Is the behavior office managed? — **Yes** →
- Complete ODR
- Email details to Administration
- Administrator determines consequence
- Administrator or designee follows through on consequence
- Administrator provides teacher copy of ODR

Intervention #1
- Conference with student
- Teach/Reteach skill
- Document intervention on sheet

Intervention #2
- Conference with student
- Teach/Reteach skill
- Document new intervention on sheet
- Communication with Parents required

Intervention #3
- Conference with student
- Teach/Reteach skill
- Document new intervention on sheet

Intervention #4 (within 6 weeks)
- Complete an ODR.
- Attach tracking sheet to ODR.

Administrator provides teacher copy of ODR

Minor Behavior: Classroom Managed	Major Behavior: Office Managed
• Preparedness	• Weapons
• Calling Out	• Fighting or Aggressive Physical Contact
• Classroom disruption	• Threats-written or oral
• Refusal to follow a reasonable request	• Harassment of student or staff
• Failure to serve a detention	• Smoking
• Put Downs	• Vandalism
• Refusing to work	• Alcohol/Drugs
• Inappropriate tone/attitude	• Gambling/Selling
• Toys	• Theft
• Inappropriate comments	• Leaving School Grounds
• Eating in classroom w/o permission	• Foul language at staff
• Cell phone not in backpack turned off	
• Electronics not stored and off	
• Dress Code	
• Cheating	
• Foul Language at student	*The school is not responsible for lost or stolen personal items

P practicing respect
A accepting responsibility
W working together
S safety matters

CONCLUSION

Behavior is what we do and say. Behavior occurs all the time and is systematically influenced by environmental events. Behavior is lawful and governed by principles that influence whether our behavior is maintained, increased, decreased or changed. We use this knowledge to help individuals gain skills that will be effective in social and learning environments. By understanding the principles we have discussed in this book we can set the stage for effective, proactive and long-term behavioral change.

The principles discussed in this book are based on the science of Applied Behavior Analysis (ABA) and it's the foundation of Positive Behavior Intervention and Supports (PBIS). There is much more to the science of behavior than outlined in the pages above, but this can be an inspiration to learn more and delve deeper into the exciting science of behavior and PBIS.

To learn more about school-wide PBIS and how to implement in your school please refer to the KOI PBIS Tier 1 Manual.

REVIEW

1. Behavior must be defined:
   a. In a way that makes sense
   b. In general terms
   c. With precision
   d. By including some action verbs

2. Which of the following is an acceptable behavior definition?
   a. Jerry tantrums 5 times a day
   b. When Sally lifts her hand and makes contact with someone, a child, an adult or an animal, with a force that makes that someone protest it is defined as hitting.
   c. Betty must learn to raise her hand
   d. Sally will sit appropriately in her chair during reading

3. To be effective in increasing, decreasing or changing behavior we must describe a behavior:
   a. Kindly
   b. Directly
   c. With Precision
   d. A and B

4. The Form of a behavior:
   a. Is what we see
   b. Is the reason the behavior occurs
   c. Guides the intervention
   d. Is what maintains the behavior

5. The Function of behavior:
   a. Tells us what the student is doing
   b. Predicts whether it is going to happen again
   c. Informs us about the why and the purpose of the behavior
   d. Tells us how many times the behavior is occurring

6. A behavior followed by a reinforcement:
   a. Will spoil kids
   b. Will maintain the behavior
   c. Will increase the behavior
   d. B and C

Answers: 1 c, 2 b, 3 c, 4 a, 5 c, 6 d

ACKNOWLEDGMENTS

Authors

Yadira Flores, Ph.D., NCSP – Dr. Flores leverages her knowledge and experience in schools to share culturally responsive education and behavior practices to help students prosper. As a nationally certified school psychologist she is an expert in psychological evaluations, bilingual assessments, and evidence-based learning strategies that impact teacher effectiveness and student's health and well-being.

Daniel Gulchak, Ph.D. – Dr. Gulchak's passion is sharing the good news about bad behavior to build the capacity of educators and empower students to succeed. An experienced special education teacher, he specializes in school-wide systems change including Positive Behavior Supports, classroom and behavior management strategies and leveraging technology to improve student behavior and academic achievement.

Angel Jannasch-Pennell, Ph.D. – Dr. Jannasch-Pennell is a leader who connects people and projects with meaningful results that impact the future for children and youth. Her broad experience in education comes from working directly to improve the lives of students with emotional and behavioral disorders to writing and directing multi-million dollar national and international research projects for universities, departments of education, and local schools.

Birgit Lurie, BCBA – Birgit is a Nationally Certified School Psychologist (NCSP) and Board Certified Behavior Analyst (BCBA). She is well known throughout the nation as a highly skilled diagnostic clinician, evaluator and instructor. Birgit has over 25 years of experience working with school-aged students, performing comprehensive evaluations and consultations, as well as mentoring colleagues in autism assessment, functional behavioral assessments (FBA), and Positive Behavior Supports (PBS). She can provide training in PRT, ABA, Ziggurat, SCERTS and TECCH models.

Special Thanks

Anika Bausom – Print book: cover design, graphics, layout
Matt Rhoton – eBook: cover design, graphics
Kegan Remington – eBook: layout, media integration
Friends & Family – for their love and continued support and encouragement

OUR ORGANIZATION

KOI Education was founded on the principles of disseminating **Knowledge**, **Outcomes**, and **Impact** in education.

KOI Education partners with educators and organizations to implement effective solutions that result in measurable academic and behavioral outcomes for students, teachers, and the school community. We have years of education experience providing direct services in K12, higher eduction, and business.

Our educational focus includes behavioral systems—including school-wide Positive Behavior Interventions and Support (PBIS), evidence-based teaching and learning strategies, applied educational technologies, and special education interventions.

Professional Development Training

One Size Does Not Fit All
Get the training you need and the knowledge to lead. KOI Education offers custom on-site and online training as well as consulting services. For the latest online events visit koi-education.com

Multi-Tiered Systems of Support (MTSS)
- MTSS: PBIS Training Academy
- MTSS: RTI (Response to Interventions)

Positive Behavior Interventions and Supports (PBIS)
- PBIS Leadership Academy
- PBSS (Positive Bus Safety System)
- Introduction to PBIS
- PBIS Assessment Coordinator Training
- PBIS SWIS Facilitation
- PBIS SET Evaluation
- PBIS ISSET Evaluation
- PBIS SET Training
- PBIS ISSET Training
- PBIS en la Casa / PBIS in the Home
- PBIS TLC Institute – Tier 1
- PBIS TLC Institute – Tier 2 & 3

Classroom & Behavior Management
- Classroom Management Teachers Toolbox
- Essential Classroom Management Strategies
- Differentiated Instruction for Today's Learners
- If All You Have is a Hammer, Everything Looks Like a Nail
- Powerful Proactive Practices to Prevent Classroom Chaos
- Responding to non-Responders and Challenging Behaviors
- Crucial Tier 3 Interventions for Classroom Management
- Behavior Principles

Trauma Informed and Culturally Responsive Practices
- Trauma Informed Care
- Using PBIS to Help Organizations Become More Trauma Sensitive
- Self Care is not Selfish, It's Survival
- Cultural Responsiveness
- Closing the Achievement and Discipline Gap
- Talking with Teens
- Suicide Prevention
- Mindfulness for Educators and Professionals
- #EduPower: Applying a Thinking Design Process as Part of a PLC

Violence Prevention and De-Escalation Cycles
- Violence Prevention
- Threat Assessment
- De-Escalation Cycle

Autism, Assessment and Structured Teaching
- Characteristics of Autism: Impact on Teaching and Learning
- Assessment Academy: Curriculum and Instruction for Students with Autism and Intellectual Disabilities
- Structured Teaching and Classroom Instruction for Students with ASD and ID

Tier 2 Targeted Programs and Training
- Motivation Strategies
- Bully Prevention
- Check-In/Check-Out (CICO): Grades K–12
- Check-Connect-Expect (CCE): Grade 9–12
- Social Skills Program
- Behavior Screening
- Data Analysis for School Teams

Tier 3 Individualized Interventions and Strategies
- Behavior Tracking Tools
- Functional Behavior Assessment (FBA)
- Behavior Intervention Plan (BIP)
- Differential Reinforcement
- Group Contingency
- Peer Tutoring
- Self-Monitoring
- Wraparound Process

CONTACT US

Contact us to schedule training or for more information:

📞 480.420.6564

🖥 KOI-Education.com

✉ info@koi-education.com

⨍ facebook.com/KoiEducation

🐦 twitter.com/KoiEducation

▶ youtube.com/user/KoiEducation

NOTES

NOTES

NOTES

Made in the USA
Las Vegas, NV
16 April 2021